IMAGES
of England

AROUND
THORNBURY

Castle and Church, Thornbury.

IMAGES
of England

AROUND
THORNBURY

Tom Crowe

On behalf of Thornbury & District Heritage Trust

TEMPUS

The church at Church End, Charfield, a little-known area of the district, *c.* 1910.

Frontispiece: This is the view that would have greeted the visitor to Thornbury Castle in the sixteenth century, with the inner arch of the main gate, which is on the north side, framing the parish church and the castle. Today the castle is approached from the south or town-side.

First published 2003

Tempus Publishing Limited
The Mill, Brimscombe Port,
Stroud, Gloucestershire, GL5 2QG

© Tom Crowe, 2003

The right of Tom Crowe to be identified as the Author
of this work has been asserted in accordance with the
Copyrights, Designs and Patents Act 1988.

British Library Cataloguing in Publication Data.
A catalogue record for this book is available from the British Library.

ISBN 0 7524 2926 4

Typesetting and origination by Tempus Publishing Limited
Printed in Great Britain by Midway Colour Print, Wiltshire

Contents

Thornbury High Street in the 1920s. Just visible beyond the motor car, a man is working on an upstairs window of the shop occupied by Mr Ogborn, the butcher. The ladder looks very precarious. The car, registration KT722, appears in a number of pictures, usually outside the White Lion, and it may have belonged to the landlord or to a regular patron.

Acknowledgements

The compiler wishes to express his gratitude to the following people and organisations for the loan or gift of the pictures used in this book and for their help in providing information about those pictures: Mr R.F. Adlem, John Adnams, Mrs Maureen Barrington, Mrs D. Brown, *Bristol Evening Post*, Mrs S.A. Clease, Gazette Newspapers, George Ford, Eric Garrett, William Grey, Mr and Mrs Roger Hall, Lyndon Hawkins, Miss J.D. Higgins, Roger Howell, Mrs Mary Isaacs, Bob Jordan, Alan Knapp, Mrs Pam Lewis, Mrs N. Niblett, Olveston Bowls Club, Olveston Parish Historical Society, Mrs M. Sealey, Mrs J. Strong, Mrs Amelia Tout, Mrs Diana Ross, Mrs J. Vizzard and colleagues in Thornbury & District Museum.

It is often hazardous to thank individuals by name for their contributions because there is always the risk of offending others, but I feel I must make special mention of Eric Garrett of Olveston, Roger Howell of Bagstone and Alan Knapp of Oldbury-on-Severn for their invaluable assistance.

We have endeavoured to locate the origin of all the pictures and to seek permission for their reproduction. We apologise to anyone we have missed in this search and hope that we have not given offence.

For many of the names given in the captions we have had to rely on the memories of our contributors, sometimes more than fifty years after the event, and inevitably there is the risk we have made mistakes. We offer our apologies to anyone whose name we have got wrong and ask you to get in touch so that we can, at least, correct our records.

To contact the Trust, please write to:
Thornbury & District Heritage Trust,
Town Hall, 35 High Street,
Thornbury, Bristol, BS35 2AR
Or via e-mail to: enquiries@thornburymuseum.org.uk

Introduction

This book arose from numerous enquiries to the publishers as to when they were going to produce a volume on Thornbury. We are only aware of two previous books in any way similar to this one, the first, in 1977, being a series of essays with photographs, covering only Thornbury, and the other, in 1987, being a book of old photographs covering Thornbury and Berkeley and some of the villages between or nearby. Both are long out of print. This present volume has been prepared on behalf of the Thornbury & District Heritage Trust for the benefit of the Thornbury & District Museum.

It may seem a little strange at first to see that this book covers not only the villages close to Thornbury but also more distant places, such as Charfield and Severn Beach, places which have, perhaps, little obvious affinity with Thornbury. This is explained by the fact that the Museum's collecting area covers the western part of the new Unitary Authority of South Gloucestershire, some fourteen parishes in all. Since the Museum is concerned with all these parishes it seemed only right that as many as possible should feature in the book. We hope that, in including some of the more distant places, we are not offending others who may feel a strong sense of ownership of those places.

When it was decided to compile this present book we were conscious that, while the Museum holds a modest archive of local photographs, the range of subjects was not great and the quality of the older images was, in general, not very high, in contrast to the images apparently available in many other places.

This quality issue is a little surprising, given that there have been several professional photographers trading in and around Thornbury since Victorian times. None of these professionals seem to have taken pictures of the locality as a hobby, unless of course such pictures have not survived or just not yet come to light. Maybe this book will, belatedly, flush them out! We hope so.

As a result of these deficiencies, a considerable amount of time has been spent in seeking suitable pictures. It is hoped that our readers will find the results worthwhile and that the pictures will not only record times long gone by, but also serve as a spur to people to record their own memories, and the places important to them, before it is too late.

Our intention when planning this book was only to use photographs taken before 1950 and, with a few exceptions, we have adhered to that plan.

We have included a considerable number of photographs of people, particularly in groups, in part to compensate for the lack of sufficient, previously unused, pictures of places, but mainly because we know they are popular and that they are particularly valuable for those doing family history research.

We had initially hoped to present a separate portrait of each parish but this has proved to be an overly ambitious idea, the number of pictures available, and the range of subject matter covered, preclude even a modest overview for many places.

It was difficult to see a coherent order to the pictures we collected, there is no obvious pecking order other than to put Thornbury, as the largest place, first. The villages are given a chapter to themselves and we have chosen to present them in alphabetical order. The space allocated to each place is little more than a reflection of the amount or quality of material available to us and in no way reflects any sense of the importance, size or affluence of those places, even in the relatively narrow time-span encompassed by the photographic medium.

We suppose it was to be expected that Thornbury would enjoy the greatest coverage, in terms of the number of pictures available, and so it proved. However, we have found it difficult to find pictures of places away from the High Street, The Plain and Castle Street, the three principal parts of the town. We have endeavoured to present only pictures that have not been used previously and we think we have almost succeeded.

It is common for books of this type to include a historical overview of the place concerned. We will not attempt this, in part because of the size of the district covered, but more importantly because we don't feel we could do it justice in the space available. There is little published material dealing with the history of the district, to which we could draw the reader's attention, so we are left to give a very brief description of the topography and industries of the area and to leave the illustrations to portray the people and places, in what will inevitably be an incomplete picture.

In an effort to make good this lack of historical information we have established a Research Group to foster research by individuals and to co-ordinate their activities for mutual benefit. Our long-term aim is to publish a history of our area. The Research Group is open to anyone who is, or would like to be, actively pursuing historical investigations, and membership is entirely free. Contact details for the Museum can be found on page 6 of this book.

The collecting area of the Museum includes Shepperdine, Charfield, Rangeworthy, Almondsbury, Severn Beach and all points between. Until the last three or four decades of the twentieth century, the district's economy was based largely on agriculture and the trades which supported it. Coal mining was carried out on the eastern fringe, in Rangeworthy, and there was quarrying for limestone, notably at Alveston, Tytherington and Cromhall. There were no major employers until modern times. Until mechanisation reached the farming community, the farms themselves were possibly the biggest employers.

The agriculture of the Vale is predominantly based on dairy farming, whilst on the higher ground to the east there are more arable farms. Sheep were not as common here as they were in the Cotswolds. Much is made in the press, from time to time, of the salmon fishing that was carried on from Aust to the northern limit of our district, and beyond, but in truth, whilst it added interesting diversity, it did not have a major influence on the local economy.

One
Thornbury

Thornbury is the only town within our district and has probably been the largest settlement in the area throughout history. Saxon in origin, the centre of the original settlement was probably close to where the church and castle are. The town only developed on the southern side, moving up the hill as it grew, so that the church and castle are now on the edge of the town.

Though it is only a small town, Thornbury is particularly fortunate in the richness of its architectural heritage. Many of the ordinary buildings, built and altered over the centuries, have survived to create the character of the town today. It was a medieval market town, one of a small group in southern Gloucestershire, and some examples of medieval buildings have survived, for example 'Porch House' in Castle Street.

The dominant architectural effect in the town is Georgian, and this is for several reasons: some of the medieval cottages had Georgian façades added to improve the street frontage; there were many new houses built in Georgian times and finally, the Victorians continued to build in a Georgian style late into the nineteenth century.

The Victorian period had relatively little impact on the architecture of the town. What buildings there are vary in style from the Gothic chapel to the classical bank on the Plain.

Looking up the High Street, there are several motor vehicles visible, which suggests a date around 1920. Thompson's Tea Rooms are on the left. Weatherheads, the furnishers, occupy the Old Market Hall.

This view of Thornbury's church and castle, around 1905, is not much changed, though there is now a road following the line of the fence across the middle of the picture and houses have been built in the meadow, to the right-hand side.

An uncommon view of Thornbury church and castle taken from the castle garden around 1905.

Dating from around 1904, this card shows that there were a number of businesses operating at the top end of the High Street at this date. There were at least three refreshment rooms, two grocers, two pubs and a temperance hotel in this short section.

The motor car parked outside the Exchange Hotel, now the Knot of Rope, in this card postmarked 1918, is exciting considerable interest. Williams' refreshment room is on the left and advertises 'Tower Tea', have you heard of it?

At the top of the High Street a very tall cyclist poses with his machine, whilst further along the street an assistant stands outside Exell's boot and shoe shop in the evening sunshine, waiting for the next customer. Embley, the saddler, occupies the shop on the right of the picture. Posted in 1905, this picture may date from before the turn of the century.

Probably taken around 1905, this picture of the Market Hall, built in the seventeenth century, sports a poster for Humber Cycles. The shops of Yarnold, the jeweller and Frank Symes, the saddler, are prominent. Just visible above the roofs in the centre is a telegraph pole, installed behind the Post Office, presumably where the telephone exchange was situated.

Charles Sweet, the butcher, in the doorway, and his son Eric (the boy in the centre) with the staff outside the shop in Thornbury High Street in early 1928. Charles Sweet died in 1959 and the shop passed to his son. The business closed in 1965. Many Thornbury residents will know this shop as Victoria Wine, which in its turn closed down in September 2002.

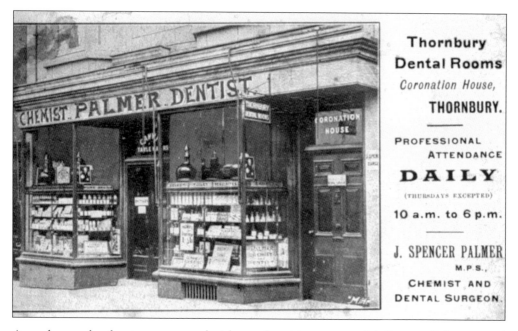

A good example of a picture postcard with an advertising message. Mr Spencer Palmer started in business in 1891 with a shop on the corner of the Plain and High Street, moving further up the High Street, to Coronation House, in 1902, where he remained until his death in 1923. This card was posted in 1908.

Possibly dating from around 1907, two men are cycling up the High Street on what must surely be a summer's day – Weatherheads are displaying deckchairs on the pavement! The Old Market Hall was still in use as a store for the town's fire-fighting equipment.

Posted in 1910, this card was photographed a few years earlier. Weatherheads are displaying their wares on the pavement but have not yet moved into the Old Market Hall. Anstey, wine and spirit merchant, occupies the building on the left, now Heritage, and Prewett, printer and stationer, still occupies the shop on the extreme right of the picture.

There are few signs of activity in this shot of the top of the High Street, which was probably taken in the early 1920s – in the window on the extreme right there is a notice concerning the 1920 and 1922 Employment Acts.

A busy morning in Thornbury High Street, possibly in the 1920s. The Old Market Hall is a very prominent landmark in many photographs of the town.

Taken shortly after 1900, this picture suggests that the High Street was almost entirely peopled by children! Perhaps they were rounded up by the photographer, since they are rather artfully placed.

The Lion and the Swan inns face each other across the High Street, c. 1905. In this view the Swan has a coronet around its neck, in other pictures the coronet is absent. It is reputed that, on at least one occasion, the swan has been removed by revellers and later found floating in a local stream. The shops of Gayner, linen goods, and Councell, grocer, with the large signboard in the centre of the picture, are prominent on the left side. There are numerous notices (possibly 'wanted' posters) on the Police Station railings.

The Castle Temperance Hotel, on the left, and the Royal Exchange as it was when this view was taken around 1900, are on the east side at the top of the High Street. Prior to 1889 the Temperance Hotel had been a licensed inn, known as the Beaufort Hotel, whilst the gabled, probably seventeenth century, building to the right was at that time called the Exchange and was a wine and spirit merchant's shop. The Beaufort relinquished its license to become the Temperance Hotel, until 1919, when it became a cinema – the Picture House. Owned and operated by the Grace family throughout its forty-year existence, the cinema closed in 1959. The Exchange obtained a license to become an inn, successive name changes seeing it called the Royal Exchange – the Exchange, again, and now the Knot of Rope, with the Stafford Knot as its sign.

The staff of Thornbury's International Stores line up for what seems to have been their annual photograph, this time in 1927. From left to right: -?-, -?-, Miss Lawrence, Mr Pool, manager, Mrs Young, Doreen Tilly, Donald Hughes.

The Old Bank, with an early bus parked at the pump, which acted as the bus terminus for a number of years, *c.* 1910.

The creeper clad frontage of the bank, facing across the Plain, is the dominant feature of this view down Castle Street, taken just before the start of the First World War. Built in 1861, the bank stands on the site of the White Hart Inn.

Thornbury, The Plain and N.P.Bank.

The Plain and Castle Street, after the town pump was removed in 1924. The BRISTOL arm of the signpost on the left carries the A38 route number, suggesting this picture was taken before the Grovesend to Falfield section of the Bristol-Gloucester road was improved in the 1930s. In later pictures the signpost carries a 'B' route number.

The Plain and John Street, Thornbury

Seen here from the bank, looking towards St John Street, the pump was such a major feature of the town and appears in many of the photographs taken before 1924 when it was removed, much to the annoyance of the residents.

A view from the National Provincial Bank across the Plain to St John Street, in the mid-1950s. Just recognisable in the centre of the picture is Trayhurn's butchers shop on the corner of St John Street and St Mary Street.

Taken in the early 1900s, this view across the Plain shows the buildings on the east side of Castle Street. The building beyond the iron railings of the pump was (and still is) a solicitor's office and housed the County Court Office at this time. The shop in the centre is Savery's, the ironmonger, still in business today.

Mr Harry Trayhurn in the doorway of his pork-butcher's shop on the corner of St Mary Street and St John Street, Thornbury, *c.* 1920. Today's public health inspectors would have a field day! The most common recollection of this establishment is of the slaughterhouse in St John Street.

The interior of Savery's ironmongers shop held an amazing array of goods – black grate-polish, shot-gun cartridges, wire netting, coal scuttles, copper and enamelled kettles and myriad other items. They also sold lamp oil and were agents for the Cyclist's Touring Club. Of uncertain date, this picture may date from around 1920.

Thornbury Grammar School was established on the Gloucester Road site in 1880 and extended in stages. From left to right, the Headmaster's house, 1906 building, 1880 building, 1909 building. The 'new' block, off the picture to the left, was added in 1932.

The Assembly Hall and classroom block added to Thornbury Grammar School and opened in 1932, pictured here soon after completion.

Thornbury Grammar School, Fifth Form, c. 1934. From left to right, back row: Lyndon Hawkins, Roger Pullin, Donald Brooks, ? Wakefield, Eric Bryant, David Morgan, Eric Eddington, Kenneth Moody, Tony Daniels. Second row: Mary Champion, Nancy Eacott, Katie Maggs, Joan Higgins, Irene Northover, Joyce Layton, Ivy Carter, Dorothy Phippin, Miss Barlow. Third row: Elsie Hobby, Heather Keir, Monica Croome, Muriel Boyt, Peggy Wilcox, Beryl Varney, Vera Sellman. Front row: Peter Briscow, Cyril Wannacott, Kenneth Pennington.

Thornbury Grammar School staff, c. 1934. Left to right, back row: Miss Tanner, Mr Pollard, Miss Smith, Mr Rabley, Miss Tomlinson. Front row: Mr Morse, Miss Dicker, Mr Jackson, Headmaster, Mr Laycock, Miss Barlow. Mr Stafford Morse was a keen local historian and was instrumental in setting up the Society of Thornbury Folk in 1946 and was its secretary from inception until he retired due to ill health in 1968. He died shortly afterwards. Thornbury Museum exists as a direct result of his efforts and enthusiasm.

The pupils of the Council School, Thornbury, photographed in 1897 or 1898. The names of only two of the children in this picture are known; they are eighth and ninth from the left in the second row from the front and are Albert Ford and his younger brother, George. George Ford went on to become the landlord of the Barrel Inn in Silver Street and Albert became licensee of the Wheatsheaf in Chapel Street. Note the schoolmaster's trousers tied below the knees with cords known as 'yorks'. It is said that farmers used yorks to prevent rats climbing inside their trouser legs!

Thornbury Council School, Std 3 in 1905/06. We have no names for any of the children. Could the teacher have been Miss Dayman – the hairstyle looks familiar?

The various Friendly Societies in the district in late Victorian times held their annual fêtes in June, usually on a Monday. This picture of the Forester's Fête, from around 1900, one of a set of four pictures of this event, rewards close scrutiny for the curious array of outfits on display.

A big procession, including a large contingent of Boy Scouts, said to be part of the Peace Celebrations following the end of the First World War, makes its way down Thornbury's High Street and into Castle Street, possibly on its way to the Parish church. The picture was taken on a summer evening, probably in July 1919.

Miss Mary and Miss Ann Jenkins, with dairying equipment, enjoy a moment of humour at Hackett Farm in the 1930s. We understand that both ladies were profoundly deaf.

Mrs Macdonald, a Council School teacher, whose class of ten-year-olds was based in the old Sunday School room at the rear of the Methodist church. The corrugated iron building was originally St Paul's church of England at The Hackett. It was moved to the Methodist church when the new church was built to replace it. Mrs Macdonald left the school in about 1952.

Born in 1879, Mr Charley Davis of Thornbury was 100 years old when this picture was taken. Mr Davis started his working life as a stonemason and then became a builder and had a hand in many of the developments in the town. He was at one time a stalwart member of Tytherington Brass Band and he was still actively pursuing his hobbies of gardening and woodcarving in 1979. In the month of his 100th birthday he was busy on his latest project – making a four-poster bed.

Jack Cornock, landlord of Thornbury's Swan Inn during the 1930s, seen here with shiny boots and a horse to match, riding to join the local hunt.

Farming competitions and shows were a feature of life in the Thornbury district for many years. Here, at a Young Farmer's Show at Thornbury Market, Mr Gilbert Bryan is presenting a cup to Mrs Jessie Harding (née Sealey).

Mr Jimmy Nichols, in white coat, with pig, and Col C.E. Turner of Oldown House, with stick, indulge in some humorous banter with the crowd at Thornbury Market during a charity auction, some time in the 1940s. The pig doesn't appear to be laughing though!

Hedging and ditching competitions used to be a popular feature of country life. In this picture of one such competition, held in the 1950s, Mr Gilbert Brown is the competitor whilst the judges are, from left to right: -?-, Gilbert Bryan and William Ford.

Farmer Daniel Long, his wife Amelia and their children, left to right, Dorothy, Amelia Rose and Victor, at the doorway of East End Farm.

East End Farm, Sibland, Thornbury, c. 1906. Three of the farmer's children, Dorothy, Victor and Amelia Rose Long are feeding the chickens. The walnut tree on the right was a noted landmark and has only recently been felled. The farmhouse still stands, though the farm land is now covered by houses.

An infants' class thought to be at Thornbury Council School, c. 1906. Miss Dayman is the teacher and Amelia Long is on the extreme right in the second row from the front. Amelia, known then as Cissie, now lives in Quedgeley.

Mr William Nichols and his wife with their children, Primrose and James, photographed at the door of Sibland Farm, *c.* 1890. The farm remained in the family until 1976.

Sibland Farm from the air, probably in the early 1960s. The farm was completely demolished in 1976 in preparation for the building of the Chiltern Park Estate. The houses in Malvern Drive now occupy the central area of this view. Part of Sibland Road, in the foreground, survives as 'Sibland' and is now a cul-de-sac.

The site of Oakleaze Road estate, photographed around 1958. The lady on the tractor is Miss E. Ashcroft, daughter of Mr Norman Ashcroft, a senior teacher at the Council School in Thornbury.

The Oldown Troop in the process of embarking a train at Thornbury Station, destination unknown, c. 1912. The Oldown Troop was formed in 1905.

A picture from the Museum's archive. It is labelled 'Guardians Picnic' and nothing more is known about it. To judge by the clothes and the charabanc driver, the picture was probably taken around 1925. The location may be Cheddar, which seems to have been a popular place for such outings. The men are presumably the Guardians of the Thornbury Union Workhouse. It seems the inmates of the Workhouse were not invited. Does anyone have any information on this picture?

A boy stands obligingly to provide human interest for the photographer in this picture looking across the Plain, c. 1910. The Royal George became an inn in the mid-1800s. St John Street is off to the right and Gloucester Road, previously known as Collister Street, disappears behind the pub. Beyond the boy, Chas Symes' ironmonger's shop displays a fine array of goods on the pavement whilst just on the left-hand edge of the picture can be seen the awning and displayed buckets of his brother Gilbert's rival ironmonger's business. There were three other members of the Symes family in business in the town at this same time.

Left to right: Mrs P. Lewis, Miss Frances Savery and Mrs Davis of the Women's British Legion, on parade in May 1948 in readiness for the service of dedication for the Women's Section.

In preparation for the dedication service of the Women's Section, the ladies of the British Legion gather on the Plain on a very wet day in May 1948.

Christmas Dinner for the 6th Maritime Regiment of the Royal Artillery in Thornbury's Cossham Hall, sometime in the period 1939-45.

A group from Oldbury-on-Severn, in the costumes of a Victorian wedding, pose outside the Goods Shed at Thornbury Station before manning their floats to join the procession to celebrate Queen Elizabeth's coronation in June 1953.

'Carnival Queen' Joan Parsons, with her attendants Audrey Bryan (on the left) and Betty Pope, acknowledges the crowd on Thornbury's Plain during the 1953 coronation celebrations. Mr Gilbert Brown is the carriage driver.

A quiet summer's evening in Castle Street in about 1910, viewed towards the High Street. The Coach House of the Chantry is nearest the camera on the left and immediately beyond it, Johnny Bond's cycle shop. Just visible in the distance is the sign-board of Salmon's, the plasterer and decorator.

St Mary Street in the 1920s, the Church Institute on the right with the Royal George and the Plough in the distance. The forlorn state of the gas lamp is a common feature of a number of Thornbury pictures.

Sgt Vaughan and his family stand at the entrance to Thornbury Police Station, High Street, *c*. 1910. At that time the policemen 'lived over the shop'.

Thornbury's Old Court House, possibly known originally as the Booth Hall, was situated in St John Street, behind The Plough, and was built in the mid-eighteenth century. It became a private dwelling in Victorian times when the court moved to the police station in the High Street. It was demolished in April 1982 to make way for the Quakers Court development and the re-routing of Rock Street. This picture was taken at that time.

The older girls of Buckover Church of England School, c. 1908. We have been given some names but we cannot associate them with individuals. The names are: Lily Billet, Ella Rogers, Freda Puffy (or Duffy?), ? Pritchard, Mabel Peters, Emmie Jennings, Winnie Longman, Carrie Clark, Clara Skuse, Ginny ?, Annie Peters, Elsie Pritchard, Dorothy Ashcroft, Ruby Hurcomb, Vera Ball, Cokey(?) Jennings.

The pupils of Buckover Church of England School pose for the camera in this picture from 1920, girls outnumbering the boys three to one. In later years, pupils transferred to Thornbury Council School at the age of seven or eight. The school (known locally as the Hackett School) is believed to have closed in the 1950s, becoming a public hall and later a private residence.

Thornbury Council School Infants, c. 1923. From left to right, back row: ? Webb(?), Katie Maggs, Amy Green, Violet Hill, Joan Higgins, Leslie Thorne, Irene Allen, Kathleen Smith, Kenneth Clutterbuck, Bert Essex, Lionel Dearing. Fourth row: Joyce Legg, Joyce Poole, ? Watkins, Marjorie Bolton, Betty Williams, Reggie Noyce, ? Payne, Freda Payne (?), Queenie Carter, Gwennie Longman, Lily Livall, Peggy Savery. Third row: ? Wilmott, Phyllis Screen, Beattie ?, Poppy (or Olive?) Lambert, ? Hopkins, Beattie Bryant, Kenneth Hopkins, Freddie Hughes, -?-, George Gingell, Arthur Webb. Second row: Ethel Dixon, Betty Thompson, John Poole, Freddie Bennett, Reggie Taylor, Reggie Maggs, Clifford Allen, Clifford Smith, Eleanor Gallup, -?-, Reggie Hill, Percy Neale. Front row: Dennis Livall, Maudie Taylor, Ruby Hill, Betty Hughes, Bert(?) Webb, ? Wilmott, ? Neale, Irene Northover, Edna Savery (?).

Members of The Hackett Sunday School, photographed at St Paul's church in September 1940. We know many of the names but are not able to list them in order.

The Grammar School Girls Hockey team of 1921. From left to right, back row: Miss D.M. Mortimer, Helen Pitcher, Doris Hendy, Gerty Ashman, Ella Chapman, Phyllis Clarke, Doris (Cissie) Heard. Middle row: Dorothy Yarnold, Minnie Smith, Kathleen Fudge. Front row: Winnie Shipton, Gladys Biddle, Lucy Clement. This is the only photograph we found of a girls' sports team.

The Grammar School Boys Football team of 1921. From left to right, back row: Mr W. Rabley, Eddie Campbell, Logan Jones, Horace Grant, Aubrey Neale. Middle row: Joe Fear, ? Hobby, Ron Tucker, Hugh Tarrant. Front row: ? Watkins, Donald Higgins, Reg Perry, ? Spratt (?), Henry Thompson.

Grammar School class of around 1932. From left to right, back row: -?-, Olive Eacott, Donald Pitcher, -?-, Richard Tilley, Mervyn Burns, Nora Lewis, Miss Smith. Front row: Molly Attwell, Helen Chambers, Charlotte Biddle, -?-, Gwen Mills, Doreen Williams, Nora Trayhurn.

Thornbury Grammar School prefects and senior staff, 1957-8. Left to right, back row: John Phillips, M.W. Darlington, Roger Howell, Tony Harding, Roger Collins, David Thompson, John Drabble, Michael Gregory, James Caswell, Greville Carey, Roger Blenkinsop, John Smith, Barrie Knott, R.W.C. Collett. Second row: D.J. Morris, -?-, Margaret Shellard, Betty Jones, Pamela Bennett, Eileen Smith, Joan Jennings, Gloria Boxwell, Daphne Jeffries, Ann Jenkins, Patricia Breen, Linda Manning, Anne Clark, Gillien Jones, Jeanne Pearce, R.P. Entwhistle, -?-. Front row: Ann Beard, Anthony Nichols, Diana Watkins, Rowland Davies, Vice Captain, Mary Newman, Head Girl, Mr Hodge, Senior Master, Mr Rouch, Headmaster, Miss Cook, Senior Mistress, Brian keedwell, Elizabeth James, Vice Captain, G.H. Organ, Margaret Bracy, D.H. Price.

Thornbury Park came into the hands of the Newman family in the early eighteenth century. The house was built around the end of that century and is believed to be the 'Thornberry-park' mentioned in Jane Austen's *Persuasion*.

Situated close to the Parish church, facing the glebe field, Thornbury House was the home of the Mundy family. The houses in Warwick Place now stand on the site.

Kyneton House was the home of the Maclaine family for many years. During the Second World War it was occupied by the 6th Maritime Regiment of the Royal Artillery, as were many other buildings in the town, and became the home of Westwing School in 1960. The school closed in February 2001.

A charming, thatched summerhouse in a sheltered spot at Marlwood, photographed here in around 1905.

Thornbury Council School, *c.* 1928. Left to right, back row: Miss Smith, Teacher, Joyce Watkins, Dorothy Matthews, Gerald Pitcher, Lyndon Hawkins, Reg Legg, Irene Northover, Joan Higgins, Mr Nicholls, Headmaster. Second row: Kathleen Smith, Violet Hill, Peggy Savery, Beatrice Bryant, Gwen Longman, Frances Carver, Kate Maggs, Ivy Carter. Third row: ? Griffiths(?), Frances Reeves, Daisy Nicholls, Eleanor Gallop, Joyce Poole. Front row: -?-, -?-, Reg Noyce, Arthur Webb.

Smiling seems to have become acceptable in school photographs by the time this one, of Thornbury Council School, was taken in 1938. From left to right, back row: E. Screen, D. Thomas, Gerald Vizard, Betty Weeks, Gwen Collins, Jessie Williams, Leslie Millen, Donald Hook, Albert Payne, Hilda Jefferies, Olive Longman. Second row: Doreen Harris, Edna Skuse, ? Curtis, George Jobbins, Joyce Rosser, Eddie Thompson, Cyril Clark, Connie Sheppard, Edna Rugman, Joyce Ford, -?-, Mr Mitchell. Front row: -?-, Stanley Huckle, Eric Webb, Blakeney Poulton, David Horder, Horace Pearce, -?-, Charlie Barton, Eileen Davis, -?-, Phyllis Hill, -?-.

Olveston and Thornbury Troops of Boy Scouts on summer camp at West Bay, Dorset, in August 1928. Left to right (O = Olveston, T = Thornbury), back row: Frank Edwards (O), Stanley Lansdown (O), Stanley Clifford (O), Bill Grosvenor (O). Second row: Joe Caswell (O), Captain Kee, Scoutmaster, Dick Tilley (T), -?-, Eric Eddington (T), -?-, Lyndon Hawkins (T), Ralph Frost (O), Victor Parsons (O), Leslie Hawkins (T), Billy Poole (T), Colin Rhind, Assistant Scoutmaster. Third row: Howard Lewis (T), Ted Parker (?), Ray Salsbury (T), Eric Pope (O), Jack Lansdown (O), Walter Burns (T), -?-, Jack Nation (T), -?-, -?-, Fred Gould (O). Front row: Peter Grove (O), -?-, Peter Barker (T), Bruce Allen (O), Bert Wilkins (O), Ted Greves (O), John Leakey (O), Ernie Grosvenor (O), -?-, Lionel Dearing (T).

M.V. Mogg, affectionately known as 'Moggy', pictured with his Thornbury Troop of Wolf Cubs. Mr Mogg ran a toyshop on the west side at the top of the High Street, where the pedestrian crossing is now.

The now traditional family group after the marriage of Miss Florence Agnes Wiltshire to Mr Frederick Rose at Thornbury Baptist church, 28 August 1914. Mrs Minnie Riddiford, the bride's sister, and Mr Alfred Riddiford are at the far right on the back row. Winifred Riddiford is sitting on the ground in front of the groom and Charlie Riddiford is on the grass at front right.

George Ford, landlord of the Barrel Inn in Silver Street, Thornbury, with his wife Elsie, behind the bar of their pub in July 1956. Note the upturned funnel on the bar, used for filling customers' flagons at the end of the evening, the flagons were to be taken to work on the following day. The white pottery mugs were for the cider drinkers.

Two

The Villages

Contained within a relatively small geographical area, the villages present, unsurprisingly, a close similarity to each other. This would have been even more apparent before the twentieth century, but now some places are experiencing considerable growth, with the demand for housing causing building in new styles and with alien materials, though most places have managed to retain their original core.

As noted in the introduction, we are not able to deal equally with all the villages, so we show here the best selection of pictures we could find, presented village by village, in alphabetical order. We had hoped that we would find a large number of pictures of farming and other rural activities but we have found surprisingly few. Many of the places shown will be quite familiar, but there are some views which might not be so well known.

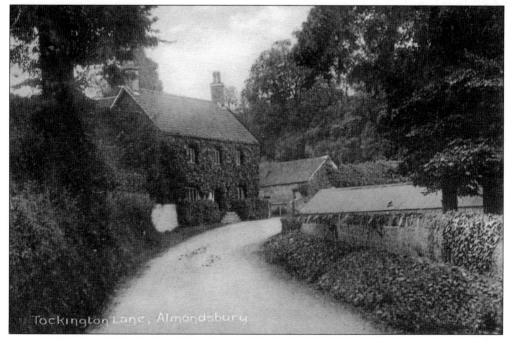

Tockington Lane, a picturesque corner of Almondsbury, *c.* 1910.

View from Almondsbury Hill

Children providing foreground interest in yet another view, this time taken from Almondsbury Hill, looking north along the Gloucester Road towards the Cottage Hospital in around 1905. The view is still recognisable today, the road being the only thing to have changed significantly, though the larger trees and the hedgerows give a less open feel today.

Almondsbury Hill.

The junction of Over Lane and the Gloucester Road, at the top of Almondsbury Hill, seen here in a postcard of around 1910, has seen numerous road-widening schemes over the years.

Though there is a motor car parked there, the Old Swan Hotel at Almondsbury still catered for horse traffic when this picture was taken in around 1910 – the sign over the door on the right is still advertising 'good stabling'. Much of the building has since been demolished.

This view, from around 1908, taken at the top of Almondsbury Hill, looking across the Gloucester Road, is easily recognised today.

Only the tower of the 'old' St Helen's church at Alveston remains standing today, the rest having been demolished after being abandoned when the new church was built nearer to Alveston village, in Victorian times. This picture dates from about 1920.

This view of Alveston, around 1910, is still recognisable though the quarry in the foreground has been filled in and there is now a children's playground on it.

The Masons Arms, Rudgeway, *c.* 1910. The inn sign reads 'Masons Arms by F. Smith. Not to sell on Sundays.' It is probably Frederick Smith and his wife standing to the right of the doorway, with the staff and a delivery man nearby. The vehicle on the right belongs to Ogborn, Purveyors, of Thornbury. The cottages are now part of the pub giving a still recognisable exterior, but the interiors have been heavily altered.

There are numerous pictures of the Ship Inn at Alveston, many of which convey a very stark, suburban feel. This one, taken before 1910, presents a more rural image, though the hedge around the pub is very tidy! A noted coaching inn, the Ship is probably of considerable antiquity.

The strategically placed pony and trap, the group of children sitting on the grass, the trees in full leaf and the church tower peeping from behind a tree evoke a sense of high summer and memories of a long vanished England. This picture of Aust was taken around 1910.

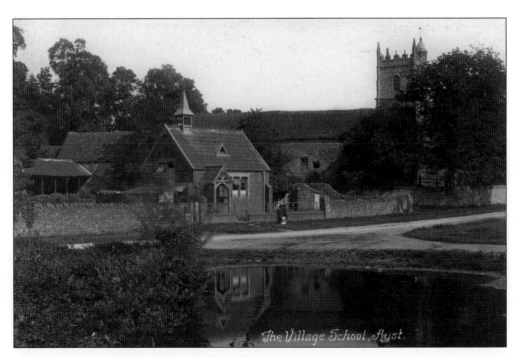

Aust church, the home farm barn, the village school and the duck-pond portray the archetypal, English village in this picture from about 1920.

The Boar's Head Inn at Aust would have benefited greatly from its position on the main route to the Aust to Beachley ferry, until the opening of the first Severn Bridge in 1966. The sign on the right suggests there was a tea garden at the inn and there is a sign for teas at a house in the distance. The picture was probably taken around 1933.

Pictured near Aust Wharf, at the foot of the Cliffs, Roland Norris sets off to begin salmon fishing in 1932. Ted Olive stands with the lead horse.

The title of this picture conjures up images of sand and sea, somewhat different from the reality of the Severn mud. Just visible in the centre of this pre-1914 picture of Aust, is the jetty later used by the Aust to Beachley ferry service. There is, as yet, no Severn Bridge or power cable that will dominate this view in the future.

Aust Pier in close-up, around 1920, some forty years before the Severn Bridge was built. The pier, which was steadily developed over the thirty-year life of the car ferry, became very familiar to many motorists. The pier was built in the first half of the nineteenth century.

Passage Hill and Aust Wharf, c. 1910. The buildings on the right were connected with the sail and steamboat ferries prior to the closure of the ferry when the railway came to New Passage in 1863. The road along the wharf had to be widened to accommodate the sightseers who came to see the first Severn Bridge under construction.

Photographed in around 1963, the car ferry at Aust was in operation from 1931 until 1966, when the opening of the first Severn Bridge made the ferry redundant.

Charfield Market's vehicle park, *c.* 1910. The horses with their carts are lined up with their noses into the hedge, so they got a free lunch whilst the farmers attended the market. The wagon on the right has hay-ladders fitted.

In the foreground a horse with wagon waits for its load. The lorry in the background suggests a date in the 1920s.

Charfield Market seems to have been held around the Railway Tavern, spilling, as in this shot, across the Wotton road. The motor vehicles suggest a 1920s date.

Watsome Bridge, between Charfield and Wotton-under-Edge, c. 1910. Few people today will be aware of this bridge, though they may pass over it frequently.

Underwood Farm, Charfield, *c.* 1900, with members of the King family. The short-horn cattle, shown here, were a popular breed on Gloucestershire farms at that time.

Milking time, old style, at Underwood Farm, Charfield, *c.* 1900. Note the woman wearing her sun-bonnet.

A pony grazes quietly whilst the driver delivers to the house with the open door, or perhaps takes a drink at the Red Lion Inn, Cromhall, in around 1920. The tree at the crossroads would survive for another thirty years.

The hill out of Cromhall on the Tortworth road in the early years of the twentieth century. Note the large slabs of rock sticking up through the unsealed road surface.

A splendid tree stands at Long Cross near the Red Lion Inn, in Cromhall, *c.* 1900. The increase in motor vehicle traffic after the Second World War forced its removal in the 1950s.

Sodom Mill, Cromhall, also known as Musty's Mill, makes an idyllic scene in this picture which probably dates from around 1905. The mill building is still in existence and has been well maintained, and is now a private residence.

Cromhall school, c. 1910. A small group of pupils stand to attention for the photographer whilst a much larger group waits impatiently on the right for the photographer to finish so they can return to play.

Pictured here in around 1905, Mount Pleasant chapel at Falfield still exists and, apart from the road having been sealed, the view is little changed today. The chapel was closed in the 1960s and the building sold.

The pupils and staff of Hill School line up across the road for this picture, taken around 1910. The building still stands but is now used as the village hall.

Advertising 1905 style. Taken at Lower Farm, Itchington Moor, for a London firm making artificial fertilisers, to advertise their product. The firm's agent was Mr William Cornock of New House Farm. The photograph purports to show what a wonderful crop of mangolds could be grown using the fertiliser. Left to right: Amelia Godsell 1863-1939, Herbert Pearce 1865-1952, farmer, -?-, Francis Bell 1870-?, -?-.

A procession, believed to be in celebration of King George the V's Silver Jubilee in 1935, rounds Wilkins Corner, Littleton-on-Severn, led by Bobby Essex.

Littleton-on-Severn, *c*. 1920. Views of Littleton are not common. The man with the bicycle and the one leaning by the wall to the right of the washing are both watching the photographer intently. The open, top-hung, windows of the cottage on the left are unusual.

Elwin Howell, farmer, 1880-1946, son of Charles and Tryphena Howell, seen here around 1930 at Maypole Farm, Lower Morton, Thornbury.

Charles Howell, 1859-1937, farmer
of Duckhole, Lower Morton, with
his wife, Tryphena Screen, 1855-
1935. Charles was the son of
William Howell of Duckhole.

Richard Howell, 1863-1936, at Yew
Tree Farm, Kington, c. 1928. The
horse on the left was named
'Limbrick'.

Sir Stafford Howard seems to have bought a pair of trousers at this fête, held in Oldbury Rectory Garden, *c.* 1915. Lady Howard is looking at the item with some amusement.

Lady Jenkinson, thought to be in widow's weeds, in the centre of the picture, attends a fête in Oldbury Rectory garden, *c.* 1915. Lady Howard, in white, is on the right.

Sarah Jones, 1796-1879, daughter of William Jones of Littleton. Sarah married William Beard of West End Farm, Oldbury-on-Severn. After her husband died she moved to Thornbury and was frequently seen thereafter riding a white horse around the country lanes.

Possibly the oldest photograph in the book, this ambrotype of Laura Cornock, aged five, was taken in 1858. Laura was the daughter of James Comely Cornock of Manor Farm, Shipperdine. She married Frank Willcox and later lived at Camp House, Oldbury. She died in 1949, aged ninety-six.

Robert James Willcox, 1878-1952, son of Frank and Laura Willcox of Camp House, Oldbury, c. 1898. Leaving school in 1893, he worked for a year in a grocer's shop in Thornbury, then taught for three years at the Thornbury Board School in Gillingstool before fulfilling his ambition to go to sea. He worked his way up to captain and took part in the tea clipper races between London and Shanghai. He sailed round the world three times, finally being persuaded to leave the sea in 1913 after the birth of his second child. He settled down to farming at Cromhall, then at Tytherington. He assisted in setting up Thornbury Sailing Club in 1947.

John Alfred Aspland, 1858-1942, Headmaster of Oldbury School 1880-1923, with his wife Mary Comely Cornock, daughter of James Comely Cornock of Manor Farm, Shipperdine, and their daughter Christabel, around 1904.

The churchwardens, choir and Sunday school teachers of Oldbury-on-Severn pose near the vicarage in 1885. Left to right, back row: Robert Knapp, Charles G. Bruton, J.A. Aspland, Miss Hannah Knapp, Mr Henry Russell, John Allen, Miss ? Cornock, Sam Bennett, Tom Knapp, Miss Leah Cornock, Miss Rosa Cornock. Second row: Miss Alice Bartlett, Miss Lily Morgan, Miss Ida Knapp, William Phipps, Revd George Fox, Walter Comely, Miss Polly Riddle, Miss Kate Thomas, Miss Nellie Morgan. Front row: ? Comely, William Phipps, ? Reeves, Levi Clutterbuck, William Knapp, ? Comely, Edwin Thomas.

Men's Bible class, run by Mrs Wilkins, wife of the Revd H.R. Wilkins, vicar of Oldbury 1887-1892, photographed at Oldbury School, *c.* 1894. Only two names are known – back row, extreme left, Robert Willcox and front row, extreme left, Bert Thomas.

The crossroads in Oldbury village, *c.* 1910. The Ship Inn is in the centre of the picture, in the distance.

The road junction at the 'Sheepwash', Oldbury-on-Severn, *c.* 1910. The gentleman on the right is thought to be Mr Clutterbuck, a well-known local inhabitant. The bungalow on the right has been demolished and replaced by a new one.

The crew of Hinder's steam lorry pose casually with their simmering vehicle at their base at Duckhole. The main business was hauling stone from the local quarries. The picture probably dates from the 1920s.

Ken Poole (with salmon) and Jim Bennett, with Tom Jones' dog, Rastus, at their fishery between Littleton and Cowhill Pill.

Richard Knapp, with kipes, at his salmon fishery at Curtis Weir, c. 1914. This fishery would later be lost to the building of Oldbury Nuclear Power Station.

Forming a near-perfect reflection, Richard Knapp and his dog pose for the photographer at Curtis Weir, c. 1914. The bank of kipes is capable of catching all manner of fish, from large to small. Richard is carrying a hoop net for catching salmon trapped in pools left by the receding tide.

Elsie Cornock Willcox, 1891-1983,
daughter of Frank and Laura Willcox, at
Camp House, Oldbury-on-Severn, c. 1938.
Miss Willcox taught at Rockhampton
School from 1910 to 1917 and then at
Oldbury School from 1917 to 1952.

Allan Knapp with his mother and sister in
their special cart, en route to his first day at
school, Oldbury-on-Severn, 1930.

A member of the Willcox family, possibly Elizabeth (1792-1865), wife of Robert Cam Willcox and daughter of John Taylor, salmon fisherman of Oldbury. The picture was taken around 1860 by Henry Dix Willcox, her husband's nephew, who lived at Olveston.

Alexander Sutherland, whose advertisement, from the reverse of one of his pictures is shown here, was Thornbury's only professional photographer between the years 1877 and 1891. We have found only two of his pictures to date, one of which is included in this book, and would like to find more, especially the landscapes he advertises here.

PORTRAIT & LANDSCAPE PHOTOGRAPHER

A. SUTHERLAND.
PHOTOGRAPHER.
GLOUCESTER ROAD
THORNBURY.

NEGATIVES KEPT
COPIES MAY BE HAD

N⁰

ANY PORTRAIT ENLARGED TO LIFE SIZE AND
PAINTED IN OIL OR WATER COLORS TO ORDER.

The owners and staff of Brutons of Oldbury-on-Severn – builders, carpenters and wheelwrights among others – pose around 1910 outside the firm's premises, which are still in use, but occupied by Mr Allan Knapp and his son Ian. From left to right, standing: Charlie Bruton, Tommy Vizard, -?-, -?-, -?-, -?-, Jack Cornock, -?-, -?-, -?-, -?-, Luke Allen, Charlie Poole. Seated: Eli Bruton, Tommy Williams, -?-, G. Jones, Jim Bruton.

Pile driving, 1911 style, at Oldbury Pill. No machinery here, just raw muscle power! The works being carried out are for the control of flooding in the village.

Smartly-dressed children stand obligingly in the middle of the road for this picture of West End Cottage, Oldbury, taken around 1910.

The Knapp family, of Salmon Lodge, Oldbury, and friends, in around 1933, with their cart which was specially built to work along the narrow footpath on the top of the riverbank. The pony's name was Johnny Jones.

Harvesting oats at Lower Farm, Cowhill, *c.* 1900. This would look very different today – no stooks, just rows of straw from the combine harvester, and far fewer trees, with the loss of the elms in the 1970s. Robert Allen, son of the farmer, Frederick Allen, is on the left.

The older boys of Oldbury school practising the basic skills of gardening in 1926. From left to right: Carey Rugman, Ernest Hopkins, Joe Rugman, Arthur Williams, Wilfred Morgan, Frank Willcox, Ray Lewis, Jim Allen, Bill Lewis.

This picture, believed to be of the ladies of the Oldbury branch of the WI, was taken in 1938. The house is Albion Cottage which is still standing. From left to right, back row: Mrs F. Bennett, Miss V. Nicholls, Miss M. Gazard, Mrs T. Davies, Miss M. Williams, Mrs A. Ridd, Miss G. Vizard, Mrs Tidman, Mrs V. Knapp, Miss A. Bartlett, Mrs C. Osborne. Second row: Mrs Watts, Mrs R. Clutterbuck, Mrs S. Stafford, Miss Bendall, Mrs Newman, Mrs Roper, Mrs S. Lucas, Miss A. Knapp, Mrs T. Williams, Mrs F. Riddle, Miss Riddle, Miss Willcox, Mrs Child. Front row: Mrs A. Morgan, Mrs G. Jones, Mrs P. Williams, Mrs J. Phipps, Miss M. Bruton (Hon. Sec.), Mrs Whitehead (Vice President), Mrs J. Cornock (Vice President), Miss C. Child (Hon Treas.), Mrs R. Allen, Mrs W.J. Cornock, Miss E. Knapp.

The Stinchcombe family of Cowhill, Oldbury-on-Severn, pictured on 14 June 1886, have donned their best clothes to celebrate the marriage of the youngest daughter, Celia, aged twenty, right, to Frederick Jones, a twenty-one-year-old brick maker from Henbury. Here the group are seen outside their home near St Arilda's church where they were married. It was not yet the fashion for the bride to have a white gown and veil. Celia, who had been a domestic servant in Thornbury since the age of fourteen, displays a simple floral decoration, as do her two sisters, Frances, aged twenty-two, next to her father, and Mary Ann, aged twenty-five, centre with a child. Frances remained unmarried, living with her parents at Cowhill, while Mary Ann, who had been a domestic servant in Littleton, had married a Bristol widower in early 1883. On the left are their father, James Stinchcombe, aged sixty-six, an agricultural labourer, and his wife Eliza, also sixty-six. James almost certainly worked at the nearby Manor Farm, to which his cottage was tied, and at which his eldest son had been a carter. The couple had five children. The cottage, now known as Vine Cottage, and considerably extended, still retains several features recognisable in the photograph. Then, it contained four small rooms together with the separately entered 'lean-to', the extreme right-hand end of which housed, within living memory, a pigsty. The wall in front remains unchanged, as does the bank on which the family pose. The photographer was Alexander Sutherland of Thornbury.

Oldbury-on-Severn school, *c.* 1933. From left to right, back row: Elsie Willcox, Alfie Till, John Till, David Thomas, Don Bennett, Bill Carter, Norman Skuse, John Webb, Colin Clark (?). Middle row: -?-, May Bennett, Eileen Howell, Vera Knapp, Phyllis Summers, Audrey Webb, -?-, -?-, Joan Clark, ? Skuse. Front row, sitting: Ron Stafford, -?-, Gerald Bendall, Muriel Lewis (?), -?-, -?-, -?-.

Photographed here with his delivery vehicle in around 1914, William Britton carried on his butchery business at Churchill House, Olveston, until his death in 1944.

This photograph of the Edwards family, taken at the door of the photographer's home in Olveston, is a fairly early example of Henry Wilcox's work. Working from home and from a studio in Park Street, Bristol, he was in business from the 1860s until around 1910.

Elizabeth 'Betsy' Jones, 1791-1865, daughter of William Jones of Littleton. She helped two other brothers set up a bakery at 36-37 Broadmead, Bristol, in 1808. Her nephew, Henry Jones, invented self-raising flour there in 1845. Betsy married John Taylor, an Olveston farmer in 1814. They later ran the White Hart Inn at Olveston. John died in 1843 and Betsy continued to run the inn after his death.

Mrs Williams and her daughter, Kate, daughter and granddaughter of Mr Edwin Organ, landlord, stand in the doorway of the White Hart Inn, Olveston, in around 1890. Originally a coaching inn on the London to south-west Wales route, the White Hart lost this trade with the coming of the railway to New Passage in 1863.

Church Road, Olveston, as it was in 1904. On the left is the gate to the churchyard; the building straight ahead was built in 1840 and was, at various times, the post office. The large building in the centre is the White Hart Inn and the cottages on the extreme right were originally stables for the inn. Percy Addis is carrying a yoke with two pails, while on the right Mrs Edwards stands with some of the schoolchildren.

This view of the 'assembly line' at William Gough's cart works in Elberton Road, Olveston, in 1923, vividly illustrates the rural nature of the business. From left to right: Alfred Fry, William Gough, Albert Teague and William Burgess.

Gough's cart works in 1923, showing the steam-powered saw-bench. From left to right: William Gough, Albert Teague, Alfred Fry, William Burgess and William Haskins. The business closed in the 1930s following the death of Mr Gough.

The horse bus operated by the Watkins family, seen in this heavily retouched photograph at Brandon House, Aust, provided a service between Elberton, Olveston, Tockington and Aust. In use until 1930, it was eventually superseded by a motor bus service run by the Bristol Omnibus Company.

In this photograph of The Street, Olveston, taken before 1910, a dog lies on the pavement on the left (perhaps waiting for his owner to emerge from the White Hart Inn) while, on the right, a man stands outside the old post office. Built in 1840, this building, which stands at the bottom of Vicarage Lane, was a post office until about 1900, became a post office again in 1936 and closed again (possibly for the last time) in 2002.

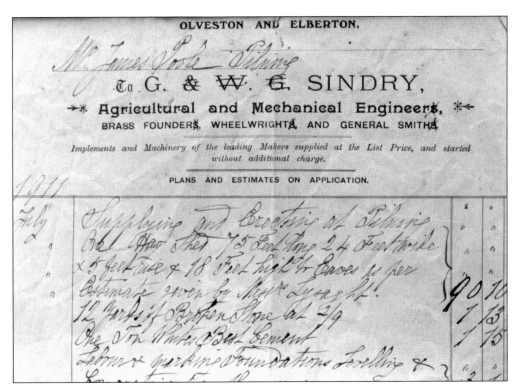

A billhead for G. Sindry, Engineers of Olveston. This is for the supply and erection of a hay barn at Poplar Farm, Pilning Street, in 1911. The cost was £90 10s.

The staff of G. Sindry, Agricultural Engineers, stand outside their workshop in New Road, Olveston, in around 1910. New Road was constructed in about 1805 to straighten out the route through the village and thereby improve the London to south Wales mail coach times.

The Street, Olveston, around 1910, some two years before the road was surfaced. Luke Pope, the road-sweeper, is on the extreme right.

The same scene as above, taken at around the same time but with a change of personnel. Only the girl remains, and she is dressed differently. She is probably the daughter of Mr Dyer, the proprietor of the shop and it may be him standing with her. The picture is remarkable for the detail in the newspaper bill below the window. It gives the headlines of the day, which include 'Terrific explosion at gas works: loss of life' and 'American railway disaster: 33 lives lost'.

The fifteenth-century gatehouse of Olveston Court.

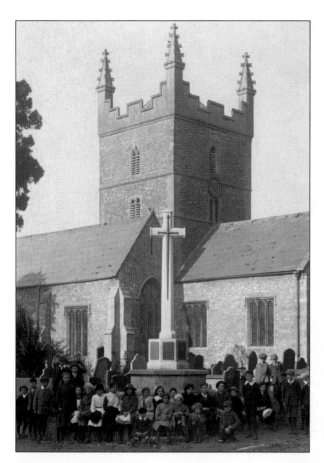

A group of local schoolchildren
gather round the newly-erected
Olveston War Memorial, in
around 1920.

'Beeboles' provided a sheltered place for woven-
straw bee skeps – this example in the garden wall
at Olveston Court is considered to date from the
fifteenth century.

The principal standing buildings of Olveston Court were built in the fifteenth century. The long wall seen here through the gateway is the remains of the twelfth-/thirteenth-century manor house of the Crok family. In the seventeenth and eighteenth centuries the Court was the home of the Sturge family, who were noted Quakers.

A quiet day in Pilning, sometime around 1910. Even the delivery van driver is sitting on the footstep of his van!

Pilning in around 1905.

Pool Farm, Rangeworthy, *c.* 1910. Mr W. Williams stands in the doorway and his daughter is in the garden.

92

The children of Rangeworthy School, 1912-13. Left to right, back row: Reginald Skuse, Fred Eacott, Edward Harford, Gilbert Payne, James Harford, Colin Powell, Gwen Ovens. Second row: Ethel Trott, Gladys Hull, Nora Amos, Dorothy Simmons, Hilda Skuse, Laura Jones, Rosie Lye. Front row: Beatrice Davis, Rose Davis, Alma Curtis, Dora Webb, Nellie Lye, Molly Eacott, Charlie Miles.

Haymakers at Pool Farm, Rangeworthy, 1915. Left to right, back row: Meshack Ovens, Len Williams, W. Williams, Mr S. Payne. Front row: Miss K. Boulton, Harold Brown, John Boulton, Mr Gleed, L. Dando.

W. Amos and his wife Nora stand in the doorway of Amos's General Stores, Rangeworthy, in around 1929.

The children of Bagstone School, 1905-06. Left to right, back row: Harold Pick, Elsie Eacott, Lily Perrett, Alice Roach, Fred Pick, William Roach. Front row: Harry Perrett, Kate Curtis, Elsie Meaken, Frank Curtis. Bagstone School was built in 1897 and closed as a school in 1922, then converted for residential use.

The children of Hill and Rockhampton, celebrating the coronation of King George V in 1911, stand on the steps of Hill Court. At the top of the steps, on the left, is probably Revd W. Coates, Rector of Hill, and on the right is Sir Herbert Jenner Fust, owner of Hill Court. Front row, on the left is Miss Eliza Jane Minerd, and on the extreme right, Elsie Willcox, both teachers at Rockhampton. In the centre of the front row Clifford Howell, aged four, is obviously worn out from flag-waving, his sister, Elsie, aged nine, is to his left.

The older children of Rockhampton School, c. 1915. Two of the girls, one sitting at the base of the tree and her sister to her right, are believed to be the children of a Belgian refugee family who lived in Thornbury.

This quiet rural scene at Rudgeway, pre-1920, looks very different today. There is now a house on the right-hand corner and a forest of traffic lights on the junction where the Iron Acton road meets the Gloucester road, which crosses the middle of the picture.

A summer scene on the beach at New Passage, taken around 1905. The jetty at the top right is the point of departure for the steamer service to Wales, run by the Bristol & South Wales Union Railway Co. The beach in this area has been altered by the raising of the banks for flood prevention.

There were many changes as a result of the First World War, but, as this picture of around 1920 shows, people still enjoyed a stroll on the beach at New Passage on a sunny afternoon. The raising of the sea wall has changed this view beyond all recognition.

Photographed in the early years of the twentieth century, Severn Beach was then a popular holiday destination for workers from the Midlands factories.

This view, of the approach to Tockington village from Almondsbury, is still recognisable though there have been many changes. The unsealed road surface indicates that this picture was taken before 1920, and possibly soon after 1900. The shop in the centre of the photograph is occupied by Leakey's bakery.

This closer view of Tockington, thought to have been taken between 1910 and 1920, shows the White Hart Inn on the right and the cottages on the left that were replaced by a garage in the 1920s.

The Green, Tockington, *c.* 1905. The stone circle around the tree was formerly a pulpit and market cross. Markets and fairs were held on the Green from the thirteenth century.

A large pile of chippings and some tar barrels, to the right of the cars, indicate that this picture of Tockington Green was taken when the road here was first sealed in 1920.

The Swan Inn, Tockington, *c.* 1920. This was a small village but it boasted three inns or beerhouses.

A meet of the Berkeley Hunt on Tockington Green, in 1904.

Taken in 1966 this picture shows the garage erected in the 1920s on the west side of Tockington Green. It was demolished in 1977 and the site is now occupied by 'town houses'.

Oldown House was the home of Col. Charles E. Turner from 1904 until it was destroyed by fire in 1953. Col. Turner was commanding officer of the Oldown Troop from its formation in 1905. The Troop was absorbed into the Royal Gloucestershire Hussars Yeomanry in the First World War. Col. Turner won the DSO with the Hussars in 1916. He was born in Scotland in 1876 and died in Olveston in 1961.

Convalescing soldiers at Tockington Manor, c. 1917. The buildings in the background were behind the Manor House and have since been demolished. The officer standing in the centre of the group is probably Capt. Pomeroy-Salmon (1865-1932) of Tockington Manor, and Emily, his wife, is probably the one nurse wearing a darker uniform. Just visible behind the nurses are members of the Thornbury Glee Club, who had entertained the soldiers.

Opening day of Oldown's sports pavilion, 24 May 1926. The pavilion was an ex-First World War army hut, acquired and converted by Col. C.E. Turner and given to the village. It was demolished in 2000 and replaced by a permanent structure.

A romantic ruin – the ivy-clad remains of the Old Mansion at Tortworth around 1900, evidence of which can still be found amongst the trees behind Tortworth church. Sir Robert Ducie purchased the Tortworth estate in 1632, but continued to live at his principal residence, Woodchester Park, staying only occasionally at Tortworth. His successors commenced the building of a new home, Tortworth Court, in 1849 and moved into it in 1853. The old mansion was left to decay.

A studio portrait of Mrs Sally (Sarah) Woodward, of the Barton, Baden Hill, dressed for market, *c.* 1900. She is wearing a sun bonnet of a type worn by women working in the fields in Victorian times. Sally carried her wares to Thornbury Market, sometimes on foot, sometimes by train.

The wedding photograph, from 1903, of Charles Ernest Skuse (1874-1951), of Tytherington Hill, and Minnie Louisa Gardiner (1877-1941), of Rangeworthy. Ernest worked at Tytherington quarries.

The girls of Tytherington School in 1892. Few names are known. They are, back row, extreme right: Agnes Rugman. Left to right, second row: Mrs Lissaman (teacher), -?-, Beatrice Bishop, -?-, -?-, Alice Cassell, Gertrude Bishop, -?-, -?-, Mary Daniels, -?-, -?-, Mary Drew. Third row: -?-, -?-, -?-, Clara Smith, Sarah Tanner, -?-, -?-, -?-, -?-, -?-, Gwen Tyler, -?-, -?-,. Front row: -?-, -?-, -?-, Susy Bishop, -?-, -?-, Gertie Lissaman, -?-.

The pupils of Tytherington School, c. 1930. Left to right, back row: Tom Cotterell, Reg Brock, Arthur Cassell, Grantley Skuse, Jeffrey Brown, Bob Willcox, Albert Day, Harry Williams, Donald Champion, Frank Niblett, Gordon Sansum. Second row: James Hemingway (Headmaster), Joan Williams, Iris Pritchard, Maude Powers, Barbara Ponting, Joan Blanchard, Donald Milliner, Ernie Cotterell, Roy Kingscott, George Day. Third row: Joan Willcox, Margaret Kingscott, Iris Wilson, Ivy Day, Phyllis Bees, Bridget Hughes, Kathleen Blanchard, -?-, Margery Woodward, -?-, Betty Boyt, Cassie Peters (teacher). Front row: Jack Skinner, Gerald Morris, Percy Reed, Ted Lival, Reg Fowler, Mervyn Weekes, Ken Phillips.

View from Tytherington Village Green, *c*. 1920. Liberty House, on the left, was the post office and shop, run by the Humphries family. To its right is Porch House, on West Street, where the Boyt Brothers ran a pork butcher's shop. One finger of the signpost gave the distance to London as 115.5 miles. Just visible on the right is the newly-erected War Memorial.

Stidcote Farm, Tytherington, 1931. Charley Davis, the well-known Thornbury builder, was engaged in altering the interior of the farm, prior to Robert Willcox and his wife Mary, née Drew, moving from Ashworthy Farm, Cromhall. Mary's mother and two aunts had lived there but had all recently died. From left to right: Charley Davis, Jim Davis, his brother, Ted Hopkins, Charlie Tandy of Grovesend.

Three
Leisure and Entertainment

We set out to find pictures that showed the numerous ways in which people have sought pleasure and relaxation. We did not succeed in finding much evidence for the playing of games, or perhaps we have simply shown that people have not photographed the games that were played. Football was clearly popular, but cricket is poorly represented, with even less evidence of bowls or tennis.

There seems to have been quite a strong interest in the performing arts, particularly music, and especially so in Thornbury. Brass bands seem to have been very popular. There is a news report of a public celebration, held in Thornbury in 1892, at which no less than six local bands combined to lead a procession: 'The enormous procession from the railway station, headed by the six united bands, marching to the strains of "See the conquering hero comes", will not easily be forgotten'.

Tytherington Cricket Team, c. 1924, pose at the Old Playing Field in Station Road. From left to right, back row: James Hemingway, Geoff Boyt, Frank Kingscott, Bill Cornock, Arthur Humphries, Truey Smith, Maurice Curtis, Austin Lival. Front row: Bert Cassell, George Edgell, Bill Curtis, Les Curtis, Hector Daniels, Alcey Curtis.

Taken at Oldbury in 1922, this group of players and spectators were involved in a cricket match which took place on the bank of the River Severn, a most unlikely setting! Fourth from the left, in the front row, is W.J. Cornock; fifth is Alfred Laver with hands on his son Harold's shoulders and second from the right in the front row is Hector Knapp.

Tytherington Cricket Team, *c.* 1894. From left to right, back row: -?-, -?-, -?-, Alsey Curtis, Bill Curtis. Front row: -?-, -?-, ? Skuse, Revd G.H. Jackson (vicar 1882-1895), Squire Hardwicke, -?-.

Anyone for tennis? Tytherington Tennis Club lay on the west side of the railway embankment between Station Road and West Street. Left to right, back row: -?-, -?-, Mr Fielding Smith of Bagstone. Second row: Mrs Arthur Boyt (?), Frederick Humphries, Florence Humphries, Morley Boyt, Phyllis Hemmingway. Third row: Cassie Peters, Gladys Morgan (coach), Mim Smith, Julia Humphries, Eric Skinner. Front row: Arthur Clements, Cis Humphries, Ivan Spratt (?).

Olveston and District Bowls Club was founded at The Park, Oldown, in 1933. This treasured drawing, which usually hangs in the Club Room, depicts in caricature some of the noted members of the club. The names are, from left to right, back row: R.A. Pitcher, Ernie Neal, George White, Jim White. Front row: George Rugman, N. Peters, C.H. Pateman, F. Oliver and H. Vokes.

Thornbury's Wesleyan Chapel Football Club of 1923/24. The building behind was used as a classroom for ten-year-olds of the Council School in the 1940s and '50s. From left to right, back row: Frank Bennett, Alf Smith, -?-, Frank Biddle, Sherbie ?, George Ford, -?-, Charlie Buckingham, Bob Mills. Second row: -?-, Alfie Davis, Percy Dyer, Nell Higgins, Lebbie Collings, Henry Thompson, Sammy Collings, Sid Vizard, Pastor Fellows. Front row: Joe ?, Joe Rugman, -?-, ? Longman.

The players in this football team seem as uncertain about the club colours as we are about the date and the team. We think the picture dates from around 1930 and we believe it was a Thornbury team. From left to right, back row: R. Saxton, Sid Rugman, J. Beaver, H. Lugg, G. Riddiford. Second row: S. Wilton, G. Vizard, I. Vizard. Front row, F. Vizard, W. Baker, Sam Collins, D. Vizard, M. Haddrill.

110

This picture is believed to be a Thornbury team of the 1950s but the date and identities are unknown.

The football team of the 6th Maritime Regiment of the Royal Artillery, which was based at Kyneton House, Thornbury, during the Second World War. Unfortunately no names are known.

Members of Thornbury Football Club at their annual dinner in the Cossham Hall, thought to be around 1950. The tulips in the vases suggest an end-of-season event.

Olveston United AFC, Bristol & District Football League Cup winners, 1932. Left to right, standing: H. Fairchild, F. Hulbert, F. Jefferies, D. Leakey, C. Jackson, N. Saxton, J. Gazzard, P. Dyer. Seated: L.Caswell, L. Jefferies, C. Neale, F. Teague, A. Fry.

Olveston United AFC, 1949. Left to right, back row: R. Gregory, L. Stovold, R. Wilkinson, W. Hills, D. Rugman, D. Lansdown, H. Fairchild. Front row: P. Lansdown, J. Hammond, R. Green, J. Caswell, C. Hook, E. Greaves.

Olveston United AFC, Bristol & District Football League, Division 4 runners-up, 1957. Left to right, back row: R. England, G. Jefferies, G. Browning, F. Curtis, T. Tilley, E. Garrett, R. Teague, B. Clare. Front row: G. Britton, M. Taylor, L. Stovold, B. Jackson, R. Lansdown.

Mrs Mundy of The Farm, Thornbury, on horseback, leading the riders at a local point-to-point. It was Mrs Mundy who, in 1937, bought The Close and its fields and presented the fields to the town for playing fields.

Photographed around 1930, Dr E.M. Grace, on the left, is riding to join the hunt. Dr Grace, who was physician, coroner and registrar was a noted personality in Thornbury for many years.

Carnival time at Oldbury, c. 1930. Sam Bennett of Cowhill, owner of this fine example of a local wagon, is seated on the shafts, in front of his name board. Tom Keedwell is riding the horse. It's a sunny day but everyone looks surprisingly glum.

A group of Thornbury ladies created a hunting scene for their float in a carnival in October 1951. Left to right: Mrs Joan Bryant, Mrs M. Stafford, Mrs M. Bennett, Mrs Roy Till, Dolly Scott, Mrs James, Mrs Cavanagh, Mrs Frances Grace, Mrs Pam Lewis.

Celebrating the end of the Second World War, this Christmas party for Thornbury's children was laid on by the ladies of the British Legion. The ladies identifiable are: Miss H. Bennett, Mrs Garrett, Miss Cogswell, Mrs M. Bennett, Mrs Phillips, Mrs Bryant and Mrs Packer.

A large crowd attended a fancy dress fête at the Mundy Field, Thornbury, to celebrate the coronation of Queen Elizabeth II in June 1953. Many names are known though it is not practical to list them. Many of those present seem to have lived in the Eastland or North Road areas.

Young men-about-town camped in the Pithay at Thornbury Castle, shortly before the First World War. Camping seems to have been more sophisticated then! All local men, they are, from left to right, standing: Claude Higgins, Norman Tucker. Seated: Bert Alsop, Godfrey Hall, Reg Phelps, Arthur Salmon.

Some of Thornbury's senior citizens at their New Year's party, held at The Castle School, in 1971.

Left: Tennis, ancient and modern – a scene from the Gloucestershire Federation of Women's Institutes Pageant held at Thornbury Castle in 1938.

Below left: Pamela Hughes dressed for her role in one of Miss Smith's operatic productions in the 1930s. *Right:* Pamela Hughes (left) and Joan Davis in costume for a Thornbury Operatic Society production, possibly *The Gondoliers*, in the 1930s.

Ken Beszant (Luiz), on the left, and Gordon Daldry (Gen. Pedro Martinez) of Thornbury Operatic Society, in a war-time production of *San Merino* at the Cossham Hall.

Charabanc outings to Weston-Super-Mare or to Cheddar Caves, as here, were very popular in the 1920s and '30s. Few names are known for this group of 1929, from Thornbury WI and the Hackett choir. Left to right, back row: Maud Worsley, Mrs Phelps, Mrs Burchell, Miss E. Ball (later Mrs Ford), -?-. Centre, front, in dark hat and coat: Miss Dollie Davis and immediately above and to the right: Nellie Hughes.

A men's outing from Oldbury to Cheddar in the 1920s. Left to right, back row: Harry Till, -?-, Robert Allen, -?-, Alfred Hopkins, -?-, -?-. Front: Robin Till, -?-, Jack Phipps, -?-, -?-. Driver not known.

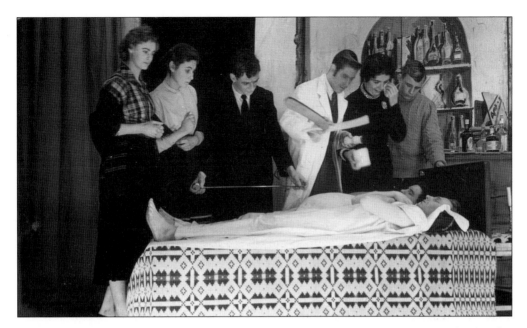

Thornbury Grammar School's production of *The Italian Straw Hat* in 1956. Left to right, standing: Elizabeth Cornock, -?-, James Caswell, David Martin, Linda Manning, Roger Howell. Lying down: ? Slade, ? Dickinson.

The cast of Tytherington's first pantomime, *Robinson Crusoe*, staged in 1952. The pantomime arose out of efforts by the vicar, the Revd Edwin Waddleton, to bring the village's Church and Chapel members closer together. The annual pantomimes continue to this day. Left to right, back row: Revd Edwin Waddleton, Jean Pitt, Charlie Oakey, Barbara English, Vera Hetherington. Front row: Ted Oakey, Beryl Pitt, Pauline Godsell, Ivy Ship, Wilf Humphries, Nan Niblett, Joan Rugman, Bill Niblett.

The orchestra of the Thornbury Brotherhood, possibly photographed in the grounds of the Baptist church. From left to right, back row: James Hobbs, Fred Dyer, Harry Smith, George Hobbs. Front row: Charles Eddington, Harry Woodward, Miss Ethel Hobbs, Charles Smith, Hector Knapp.

Ladies attending Tytherington Fête at the Old Vicarage in Duck Street, *c*. 1905. It must have been a very colourful sight – all the ladies are dressed in kimonos. There was a vogue at the time for all things Japanese. The Old Vicarage has been considerably altered since and is now called The Manor.

A fête in the Old Vicarage Garden, Tytherington, *c*. 1905. Themed dress for the ladies seems to have been a feature of such events. Three quarters of the names are known, but we will give only three – Revd H. Arkell, vicar of Tytherington, in the centre, with his two church wardens: Herbert Pearle, on his right, and William Cornock on his left, .

Taken in the summer of 1912, this picture of the Committee of the Thornbury Brotherhood was probably posed in Ogborn's Field, behind the Methodist church in Thornbury High Street – approximately where the road into Castle Court car park now is. It is believed that the Brotherhood was a men's social club associated with the Baptist Church. From left to right, standing: E. Luker, J. Allen, James Hobbs, James English, C. Collins, Mr Phillips Snr, Charles Eddington, Harry Smith, Aaron Penduck. Middle row: Sam Tottle, Robert Underhill, Miss Ethel Hobbs, George Phillips, William Liddiatt. Front row: Fred Holley, Elton English.

The Thornbury Society of Gleemen photographed at Berkeley Castle on 9 September 1897, by Charles Eddington who was also a member of the society. The group gave concerts in numerous places around the district. Left to right, seated on left, -?-, F. Smith, -?-, -?-, -?-, F.K. Howell, G. Symes. Standing at back: -?-, A.E. Bevan, -?-, H. Trayhurn, A.H. Wilkins. Seated on right: -?-, -?-, E. Brown, H.D. Boulton, H.P. Thurston. Seated at centre table: W. Yarnold, E. Eddington, C.A. Pitcher, -?-.

Tytherington Brass Band, pictured here in around 1913, was formed by Squire Hardwicke in the early twentieth century. The band twice won the cup at the annual competition at London's Crystal Palace. It was a keen rival to Listers' Band of Dursley. Squire Hardwicke owned Tytherington Quarries and when applying for a job there it was a distinct advantage to be able to play an instrument. Left to right, back row: -?-, -?-, -?-, -?-, Austin Lival. Second row: Gilbert Dutfield (conductor), Lawford Blanchard, Charley Davis, Fred Lynes (b. 1903!), -?-, George Selby, -?-. Front row: -?-, -?-, Frank Lival, Arthur Lynes, Charlie Poole.

Thornbury Baptist Prize Band, 1910. From left to right, back row: Edgar Legge, Howard Knight, Claude Higgins. Second row: Frank Williams, Ernest Phillips, Jack Phillips, William Liddiatt, James Hobbs, Hubert Baylis. Third row: Robert Underhill, Percy Liddiatt, George Phillips, Revd Young, H. Martin (conductor), Harry Phillips, George Hicks, Arthur Collins. Front row: Howard Baylis, William Champion.